Who Were The Beatles?

Who Were The Beatles?

by Geoff Edgers

illustrated by Jeremy Tugeau

Penguin Workshop

For my two favorite ladies, Carlene and Lila . . .
All together now—GE

For Nicole, my biggest
critic and biggest inspiration—JT

PENGUIN WORKSHOP
An Imprint of Penguin Random House LLC, New York

Printed in the USA.

Visit us online at www.penguinrandomhouse.com.

Library of Congress Control Number: 2005014000

ISBN 9780448439068 45 44 43 42

Contents

Who Were the Beatles?

They were known as the Fab Four. And they were so famous that if you just said John, Paul, George, and Ringo, people knew who you were talking about.

They looked different from most young guys in the early 1960s. They wore their hair longer. Reporters called them the "Mop Tops." Their

clothes were different, too. They wore collarless suit jackets, which buttoned all the way to the top. Their accents were different, too, because they were from England. Liverpool, England. Before that, all the biggest pop stars were American.

Most of all, their music sounded different. It was rock and roll, but not like anything kids had heard before. When the band came to the United States for the first time, concert stadiums sold out. People went wild. Girls fainted. Newspapers called it the "British Invasion."

They were even bigger than Elvis. Then, when they were at their most popular, the Fab Four broke up. Yet more than forty years later, their songs are still huge hits. In November 2010, it was front-page news when all thirteen of their studio albums became available on iTunes.

Who was this band? The Beatles, the greatest rock group ever.

Chapter 1
John Lennon

There was nothing quiet about John Lennon, not even the day he was born. It was October 9, 1940. World War II was raging in Europe. Liverpool, England, was being bombed by the Germans. But baby John couldn't wait. His mother, Julia, went to the hospital and gave birth at seven in the morning. As he arrived, the walls of the hospital shook from falling bombs.

Even before the war, Liverpool was a gloomy place to live. Once a thriving seaport, the rain-soaked city had become run-down. Many factories were closing and those that remained open didn't have enough jobs. Poor families were crammed into small apartments in the slums of town.

At first, John lived with his mother and grandparents. John's father, Alfred, was never around. He worked on a ship and was gone for months on end. As hard as she tried, John's mother couldn't make enough money to support her baby son. For a little over a year, Alfred sent checks home. Then the checks stopped, and Alfred stopped writing. Julia couldn't even afford to get John his own bed. He ended up sleeping in hers.

Things grew worse; John's family began to fight over where he should live. Julia wanted him to stay with her. He was her son. But she had trouble taking care of him. John's aunt Mimi also wanted the boy. She said that John would be better off with her. Mimi lived in a big house in a better part of town. John's father tried to take him, too. One weekend, John went to visit his father, whose boat had docked in Liverpool. Alfred asked the boy, only five years old, if he wanted to go on an adventure. They would travel together to a faraway country called New Zealand. "Sure," John said. It sounded like fun.

Then Julia found out what Alfred was planning. She told him to stay away. But much as she wanted John, Julia saw that her son needed a better home. In the end, she decided to send him to Mimi.

Despite all of this, John was a happy boy. Pictures from those days show him with a big smile on his face, whether he was riding his bike or standing with the family dog, Sally. Mimi gave him lots of books. Along with reading, John liked to make monsters and skeletons out of paper, and paste them over his bed.

Because John was so young, he didn't really know that it was unusual to live with his aunt and have his mother visit. Besides, Julia acted more like a buddy than a mother. She loved to tell jokes, make funny faces, and sing. She taught John how to play the banjo, an instrument similar to a guitar. From Julia, John heard stories about his banjo-playing grandfather, who had moved to the United States. It was John's mother who gave him his first guitar. She also taught him how to play it.

Aunt Mimi had lots of rules. She expected John to come home after school to do homework. She wanted him to go to bed early. She often had good reason to get mad at John. As he got older, John got into more trouble. He was smart, but he didn't work hard. He did well only in art class. John spent most of his time making little books of poems and drawings. He also got into fights with other kids. And he sometimes made fun of his teachers, even when they were right there in the room.

Perhaps he was acting up out of sadness. A few months before his eighteenth birthday, Julia was hit by a car and died. John was heartbroken. Years later, he wrote the song "Julia" about her.

As a teenager, the one thing John got serious about was music. When he was fifteen, he heard rock and roll for the first time. Until then, most music heard on the radio was soft music, sung by such stars of the day as Perry Como and Doris Day. Rock was different. The music was loud. It had a strong beat and you could jump around to it. Many grown-ups hated it. Teenagers loved it. Rock had exciting stars.

John's favorite singer was Elvis Presley. Elvis was from Tupelo, Mississippi. He had thick black hair, which he slicked up with grease. He wore his shirt unbuttoned so his bare chest would show. His jeans were very tight. And when Elvis sang, he swiveled his hips. Girls went crazy. Boys admired him. But many adults thought he was a bad influence. When Elvis went on television, he was only shown from the waist up. That way, nobody could see him dancing.

ELVIS PRESLEY

BORN IN MISSISSIPPI, ELVIS PRESLEY WAS THE FIRST REAL ROCK STAR. HE WAS A WHITE SINGER WHO CAPTURED THE SOUND OF AFRICAN-AMERICAN BLUES MUSICIANS. THERE WERE OTHER WHITE SINGERS WHO DID THIS, TOO, BUT ELVIS WAS THE MOST EXCITING.

ELVIS RECORDED HIS FIRST SONG IN 1953, "MY HAPPINESS." HE PAID FOR IT HIMSELF AS A GIFT TO HIS MOTHER. FOR A WHILE, HE WORKED IN A MACHINE SHOP AND DROVE A TRUCK. EVENTUALLY, HE WAS DISCOVERED. HIS HITS INCLUDED "HOUND DOG" AND "HEARTBREAK HOTEL."

AS HE BECAME MORE POPULAR, PEOPLE STOPPED CALLING ELVIS BY HIS REAL NAME. INSTEAD, HE BECAME "THE KING" OF ROCK AND ROLL.

John started dressing like Elvis, right down to the greasy hair. He also decided to play guitar. Mimi didn't approve. She wanted John to take piano or violin lessons, and wouldn't pay for guitar lessons. John kept on playing guitar, anyway. He was a natural. Soon, John formed his own band at school. It was called the Quarrymen.

Still, Mimi wouldn't let him in the house with his new instrument. John had to practice outside, in the garden. "A guitar's all right," Mimi told him. "But you'll never earn your living by it."

Chapter 2
Paul McCartney

To Beatles fans, Paul McCartney was always known as "the cute one." He had long eyelashes and big brown eyes and shaggy hair. He also sang some of the group's most romantic songs, the ballads. As a kid, though, Paul was chubby. His brother Michael picked on him and called him "fatty." Paul tried not to let it bother him too much. And as he got older, he started to lose his baby fat.

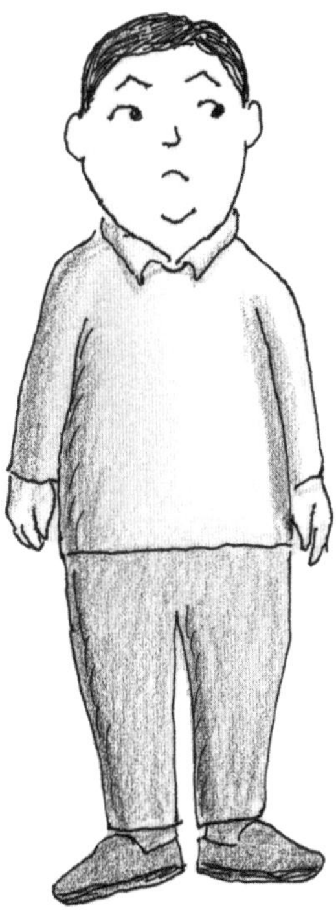

Paul was born on June 18, 1942. His mother, Mary, had a private hospital room. Poor women usually had to share a room with other brand-new moms, and the McCartney family didn't have much money. But Mary worked as a nurse, so the hospital treated her like family.

Paul was a pretty good kid. His grades were good, especially in Latin, and he made lots of friends. He liked to draw and write. He liked girls and bragged to all of his friends when he had his first kiss. He loved music, too.

Like John, Paul couldn't believe what he was hearing when an Elvis Presley song came on the radio. It sounded so different. Paul also liked Little Richard, a black singer.

Elvis was cool and handsome, but Little Richard wore bright makeup, acted wild onstage, and sang songs called "Tutti Frutti" and "Good Golly, Miss Molly." Actually, Little Richard didn't just sing. He screamed. When he played piano, Little Richard got so excited, he had to stand up. Sometimes, he kicked the piano bench away.

Paul learned to imitate Little Richard's loud yells. That annoyed most adults. Much later, those shouts became part of some of the Beatles' most famous songs, like "She Loves You" and "Twist and Shout." Paul also liked to dress up as a rock star. He wore his pants tight, and let his hair grow longer than the other kids'.

It's no surprise that Paul listened to so much music when he was a kid. His father, Jim, played piano and once led a group called Jim Mac's Jazz Band. Jim set up a radio in Paul's room so he could listen to music as he fell asleep. Paul's uncle gave him a trumpet. But Paul's favorite instrument was the guitar. Why? Because Elvis played one. Guitars were made for right-handed people, but Paul was left-handed. So, he had to restring it upside down to play it. And, boy, did he play it.

“The minute he got a guitar, that was the end,” said Michael, Paul’s younger brother. “He was lost. He didn’t have time to eat or think about anything else.” He played it while he sat on the toilet and while he was in the bath. He played it everywhere, Michael said.

Paul became even more serious about music when his mother became ill. It started with a pain in her chest.

In those days, doctors didn't have all the tests there are today to figure out what was wrong with a patient. They sent Mary home, which was a big mistake. When the pain didn't go away, Mary went back and this time, the doctor told her the terrible news. She had breast cancer and probably wouldn't live long. Mary cried when she found out, but she didn't tell her sons. She didn't want to upset them. She died on October 31, 1956. Paul was only fourteen years old.

Paul prayed that she would come back, but he knew she wouldn't. He wondered how his family could ever be the same. Overwhelmed, Paul turned his sadness into music. He wrote his first song and called it "I Lost My Little Girl."

Chapter 3
Ringo Starr

Of all the Beatles, Ringo had the hardest childhood. The oldest Beatle, he was born on July 7, 1940, the first and only child of Elsie and Richard Starkey. He was named after his father,

although his father left when Ringo was only three, and rarely returned to visit. Later, after Richard became a musician, he changed his name to Ringo Starr. A musician would often take a different name, called a stage name, because he or she thought it sounded better.

As a boy, Ringo was lonely. Elsie would watch her son stare out of the window, wishing he had a brother or sister. Then, at age six, things got worse. Ringo got sick. He felt a terrible pain on his right side—it was appendicitis. Appendicitis is easy to fix, but no one thought to take him to the doctor until he got really sick. Ringo was rushed to the hospital, where the doctor put him to sleep and took out his appendix. But after the operation, Ringo didn't wake up. He was in a coma. For ten weeks, Ringo's body stayed asleep. When he did wake up, he still felt sick. So, he ended up staying in the hospital for a whole year until he was well again.

When he finally returned to school, Ringo found it hard to catch up. He tried his best, as one of his teachers wrote on a report card. But he kept failing tests. He didn't know as much as his classmates did. What's worse, he got sick again. When Ringo was thirteen, he caught a cold that got much worse. He had trouble breathing and had to go to the hospital again. This time, he stayed for two years.

One good thing did come out of his time away from home. In the hospital, Ringo learned to play drums. The hospital had a band travel around

from room to room to play music. It was a way to cheer up other kids who were there. Ringo had always been interested in drumming. He used to tap along to the rhythm of any song he heard. Now, in the hospital, he was given a drum to bang on—and he loved it.

When Ringo went home, he built his own drum set out of metal cookie containers. He used small pieces of

firewood for his sticks. Music gave him something fun to do while all his friends were outside, playing. Also, he had fallen so far behind in his class that he didn't feel smart. He ended up dropping out of school at fifteen. But no matter what, he was really good at drumming.

Because he wasn't in school anymore, Ringo had to find a job. He worked on a train, carrying messages back and forth to people. (There were no such things as cell phones back then.) He served drinks on a boat. He got a job fitting pipes together so water could move through them. Even though he made enough money, Ringo knew he needed more out of life. He just wasn't happy.

When Ringo turned eighteen, his mother bought him a set of real drums. It was the best gift she could have given him. He practiced making a steady beat. He made the cymbals ring out when he hit them with his drumsticks. He formed a band. They were called the Eddie Clayton Skiffle Group.

The band played mainly during breaks for workers at the pipe-fitting plant. That was fine with Ringo, though. He didn't need to get rich and be famous. It was enough just to be in a band.

Chapter 4
George Harrison

George Harrison had the happiest childhood of the Beatles. He didn't have the sadness of losing his mother as Paul and John did. He didn't get sick like Ringo.

He was the youngest of four children. He was also the youngest Beatle, born on February 25, 1943. Harold, his father, drove a bus. Louise, his mother, taught ballroom dancing. But little George wasn't interested in dancing. He wasn't interested in music, either. He was a quiet boy.

As he got older, he wore tight pants and grew his hair long, even though the other kids made fun of him for it. George used to tell them he kept his hair long because the scissors his father used weren't sharp, and so every snip hurt. Of

course, that wasn't true. He just liked the way his hair looked.

Music came into George's life when he was fourteen. That's when he heard a British singer named Lonnie Donegan. The music Lonnie Donegan played was similar to rock and roll, except it was faster. They called this new music

"skiffle." George loved the sound of it, and begged his mother to buy him a guitar. She finally agreed, and bought one for five dollars.

George taught himself how to play. He practiced so much that the tips of his fingers started to bleed. Eventually, though, George got the hang of it. Soon he wanted a better guitar. An electric guitar. An electric guitar is much louder because when it's plugged in, the sound runs through a speaker. Even though the guitar was sixty dollars, his mother bought it for him.

Before long, George had formed a band with one of his older brothers, Peter. They called themselves the Rebels, and played their first show at a club in Liverpool. Soon after, George was on a bus and met Paul. They started talking about music and realized they had a lot in common. They started meeting at George's house to practice music together.

While Paul loved to sing, George was more interested in playing guitar. He was actually too scared to sing in front of people. Years later, he would be known as "the quiet Beatle."

Chapter 5
Forming the Band

When the Beatles were growing up, there was no MTV, no iTunes. There wasn't even a radio station that played rock and roll. In fact, when the Beatles were small boys, rock and roll didn't even exist!

In the United States, there was a style of music that had the same energy as rock. It was called "rhythm and blues." Black people invented that kind of music. But in the early 1950s, deejays wouldn't play their music on the radio. So for four young boys in England, there was no chance to hear the music that became rock and roll.

Instead, they were stuck listening to white people perform what came to be called "bubblegum pop." It also came from the United States. These were happy, harmless songs that were easy to sing. Parents liked them. "How Much Is That Doggie in the Window?" was a big hit in 1953. It didn't make grown-ups feel uncomfortable. But then, in the mid-1950s, music companies started to ask white singers to perform rhythm and blues. That's when rock and roll was born.

RHYTHM AND BLUES

RAY CHARLES

BEFORE ROCK AND ROLL CAME "RHYTHM AND BLUES." IN FACT, THE ROCK MUSIC MADE IN THE 1950S SOUNDED ALMOST THE SAME AS THE RHYTHM AND BLUES THAT HAD BEEN PLAYED IN CLUBS FOR YEARS. THE BIG DIFFERENCE IS THAT RHYTHM AND BLUES WAS CREATED BY AFRICAN-AMERICANS. THESE BLACK SINGERS TOOK SONGS THAT WERE

ONCE COUNTRY, BLUES, OR BIG BAND MUSIC AND MADE THEM GREAT TO DANCE TO. THEY SHOUTED, THEY SANG FAST, THEY BANGED ON THE PIANO.

SADLY, EVEN A HUNDRED YEARS AFTER THE CIVIL WAR, BLACK PEOPLE IN AMERICA WERE TREATED UNFAIRLY. RHYTHM AND BLUES SINGERS COULD PLAY CLUBS. BUT THEY COULDN'T GET THEIR SONGS PLAYED ON THE RADIO. THE MUSIC COMPANIES CAME UP WITH AN IDEA. WHAT IF THEY HAD WHITE SINGERS RECORD BLACK PEOPLE'S SONGS? IT WASN'T FAIR, BUT IT WORKED. ELVIS PRESLEY SANG ROY BROWN'S "GOOD ROCKIN' TONIGHT," AND BILL HALEY DID "BIG JOE" TURNER'S "SHAKE, RATTLE & ROLL."

ROCK AND ROLL WAS BORN. AS FOR BLACK ROCK MUSIC, IN THE LATE 1950S A BLACK RECORD COMPANY NAMED MOTOWN STARTED PRODUCING MUSIC BY BLACK GROUPS. SOME OF THEM, LIKE THE SUPREMES AND THE TEMPTATIONS, BECAME VERY FAMOUS. THE MOTOWN SOUND WAS PLAYED ON RADIO STATIONS ACROSS THE COUNTRY AND MADE STARS OUT OF THE SINGERS.

Rock's first hit came from a man named Bill Haley. It was a song called "Rock Around the Clock." Kids liked it because you could sing and dance to it. Plus, it was used in a popular movie at the time, *Blackboard Jungle*. Then came Elvis Presley. Everyone, including John and Paul, wanted to be just like Elvis.

John's band, the Quarrymen, got its name from his school, Quarry Bank. The Quarrymen played their first gig in the summer of 1957. That was also when Paul saw John's band play at a local church.

It was a warm, summer day. John stood up on a stage with his guitar and sang. Paul was very impressed by what he heard. He went up to John after the show and said that he also played music. Then he grabbed someone else's guitar and played a song to prove it. John was just as impressed by what he heard. He wanted to ask Paul to join his band, although he worried that fans would like Paul more. But John decided that Paul would help the band. They played their first show together in October. After the gig, Paul showed John the song he wrote after his mother died. John went home and wrote a song of his own called "Hello, Little Girl."

It was later that winter that Paul took his new friend George to meet John. George was only fifteen at the time. *Too young*, thought John, *to be in a band.* John was eighteen. But Paul convinced John to let George in. Now, all they needed was a drummer.

At first, they found a drummer named Colin. But he quit after a fight with John and Paul. Then, drummer number two, Tommy Moore, had to leave the band because his girlfriend wanted him to get a paying job. He went to work in a bottle factory. Then, they took on a guy named Pete Best, who was the son of a local club owner.

Finally, they wanted to bring on a bass player. (That's pronounced like "base," as in baseball.) A bass looks like a guitar, but it plays only low notes, a "bass

PAUL
GEORGE
JOHN
PETE
STU

line." Its job is to keep the beat of the song. John convinced one of his friends, Stu Sutcliffe, to take up bass so he could join. Stu bought a bass guitar and tried to learn how to play it. He didn't stay around very long, but he did do one important thing. It was his idea to change the band's name from the Quarrymen. In February 1960, the band was renamed the Beatles. The name had nothing to do with the bug—it was because their music had such a strong beat.

Chapter 6
A New Name, a New Look

Now that they were a band, the Beatles needed to book some gigs.

Back then, no one knew they'd be the most popular rock band in the world one day and sell millions of albums. No one knew they'd someday be called "the Fab Four"—short for Fabulous Four—or that they'd be able to fill baseball stadiums with fans. In those days, when the Beatles came calling, all the club owners saw were five scruffy teenagers in beat-up leather jackets.

At first, their music wasn't very good. It wasn't their fault. Stu was just learning how to play bass. And he didn't really want to be in the band, anyway. He wanted to be a painter. John never took guitar lessons, so he still made a lot of mistakes. Same

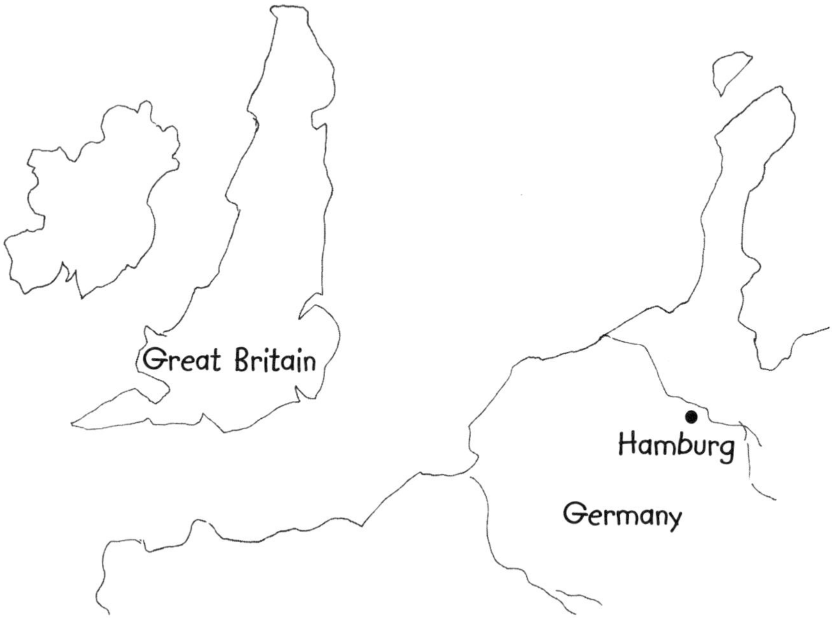

thing for George and Paul. And the only reason Pete was the drummer was because he owned a drum set.

In 1959, they got their first steady job. A club owner in Hamburg, Germany, visited England. He was hoping to find a group of cheap, young rock-and-rollers. He made an offer to the Beatles. Hamburg was far away, in another country. But the club owner promised the Beatles a place to sleep and a regular paycheck. Even their own dressing room. Naturally, the boys were excited.

Their parents, however, were not. Aunt Mimi had always opposed John's dream of playing music. Now she insisted that John stay in art school. Paul's father also put up a fight. He worried that Paul wouldn't get enough to eat if he went to Germany. But like Mimi, Jim knew he couldn't really stop his son. John and Paul were eighteen and old enough to do what they wanted. And they wanted to go to Germany.

Hamburg sounded great to the boys. When they got there, though, they found that some of the club owner's promises were lies.

The club was a dirty, smelly place called the Indra. Their "dressing room" was actually a public bathroom. They slept on small beds set up behind the screen of a local movie theater. After playing

all night, they couldn't even sleep late the next morning. The sound of the movies woke them up.

Performing onstage wasn't easy, either. In the past, their gigs lasted an hour at the most. In Hamburg, they were on stage for eight hours. But all that practice did help make them better musicians. John and Paul wrote lots of songs. They also learned how to play dozens of songs by their

favorite musicians, including Elvis Presley, Buddy Holly, and Chuck Berry. They even made up songs on the spot. That's called "jamming."

Sometimes, they felt tired and grumpy. Playing so hard and not getting enough sleep was taking its toll. They started to take pills to stay awake on stage. They couldn't eat much because they were

working so hard. Actually, they often ate while they were playing, right in front of the audience.

Their fans were interesting. Sometimes, the club would be filled with teenagers who loved the Beatles and sang along with their songs. Other times, the fans had too much beer and got into fights. They threw chairs and swung from lights hanging down from the ceiling.

The Beatles didn't mind, though. They thought that was cool.

As time passed, the Beatles became more popular and did some shows at bigger clubs. They also made a lot of friends with art school kids who gave the boys advice on how to wear their hair. In Germany, the style was to grow your hair out and comb it forward. The Beatles decided they liked this better than using all that grease. This new

BRIAN EPSTEIN

hairstyle would become what was called the Beatle "mop top."

After four months, though, the Beatles had had enough of Germany—except for Stu. He had fallen in love and wanted to stay in Germany. Everyone else went home to Liverpool, England. The Beatles had become good songwriters and musicians by then, and they liked showing off. They had no trouble getting work now. They even attracted the attention of a local

businessman named Brian Epstein. Brian came from a wealthy family. He wanted to manage a rock band. The Beatles trusted him.

Brian had different ideas about what the boys needed to do to make it big. He told them no more eating or drinking onstage. No more leather jackets. Instead, they would wear matching suits and ties. He thought that would make the Beatles more appealing to parents.

The band agreed to all of it, if Brian would do them one favor. They didn't want Pete to play drums anymore. They wanted someone better—a guy named Ringo Starr, who was in another band. John and Paul were too scared to kick Pete out. He had been their friend, and they didn't want to hurt

his feelings. So they had Brian do it. Pete never forgave them for not telling him personally.

By 1963, the four members of the band were in place: John, Paul, George, and Ringo.

Chapter 7
Beatlemania

It all happened very fast. At the start of 1963, the Beatles were still playing small clubs, or performing as an opening act for other bands.

Then, that March, their first album came out in England. It was called *Please Please Me*, and it became a big hit on the British charts. That's a list of best-selling records. Even on their early songs, the Beatles sounded special. They had two main singers—John and Paul—who knew how to perform harmonies together. Their songs always had a catchy chorus. And the band loved to yell in happiness at the end of some parts.

This spirit caught on.

By fall, the Beatles could sell out a show in half an hour. They were so popular that fans chased them everywhere. A newspaper in England came up with a way to describe this excitement: "Beatlemania."

In the United States, though, the Beatles were still unknown. Their first song in the U.S. was such a flop that their record company got rid of them. So they signed with Capitol Records. When Capitol was slow to put out a new song, Brian got on the phone and yelled at the managers. He said that "I Want to Hold Your Hand" would be a big hit. Brian was right. The song went to number one.

On February 7, 1964, Beatlemania hit America. That's when a plane arrived at Kennedy Airport in New York City containing four nervous young men. John, Paul, George, and Ringo were coming to America for the very first time.

There had never been rock stars from England before.

"They've got everything over there," George said about the United States, before the big trip. "What do they want us for?"

Brian didn't have any doubts. He kept telling everybody that the band was going to be huge. And as soon as they got off the plane, the Beatles proved Brian right. Thousands of screaming teenagers showed up to greet them at the airport. The Beatles were cute. Girls pushed themselves up against the fence separating them from the airplane. They cried when John, Paul, George, and Ringo walked out of the plane. Some of the fans even passed out when the Beatles waved.

At the airport, the Beatles held a press conference. Reporters were used to hearing polite answers from rock-and-rollers. Even Elvis called reporters "sir." But the Beatles made jokes. One reporter asked them to sing a little. "We need money first," John said, giving everyone a good laugh. Soon reporters were scribbling down every word the Beatles spoke.

Two days later, the Beatles played five songs on *The Ed Sullivan Show*. And that day, they made history. More than 73 million people across the country watched. That was almost half of everyone in the United States. When it was over, the Beatles performed many sold-out concerts, including two at the famous Carnegie Hall in Manhattan.

ED SULLIVAN

All this attention also helped other British bands become popular in America. The Rolling Stones, the Animals, the Kinks, the Dave Clark Five, Herman's Hermits, and Freddy and the Dreamers: They were all groups from England that became famous after the Beatles. The press called this the "British Invasion." Some of the other groups were also from Liverpool. The new music was called the "Mersey Sound" after

the Mersey River, which runs through Liverpool.

Beatlemania didn't just mean selling out concerts or making number-one records or girls screaming or boys wearing their hair long. The Beatles belonged to kids of the sixties the same way Frank Sinatra belonged to their parents.

In 1964, the Beatles made their first movie, *A Hard Day's Night*. A lot of the action in the

movie showed the band running away from fans. It was a big hit.

By now, John, Paul, George, and Ringo were no longer four guys from Liverpool. They were "the Fab Four," even bigger than Elvis. They were still young and inexperienced, though, and sometimes made mistakes. John once told a reporter that the Beatles were "more popular than Jesus now." Many people were deeply offended. Some radio stations held protests with big bonfires. People were invited to throw Beatles albums into the flames. John quickly apologized. But the experience changed the band. They had to watch what they said and how they behaved. Being the Fab Four didn't seem as fab anymore.

Chapter 8
Road-Weary

Being rock stars wasn't easy. When they weren't recording new songs, the Beatles were packing their suitcases to head to the next concert. There wasn't much time to rest. In sixty days in 1964, they played fifty-three concerts, each in a different city in the United States. The fans went so crazy that, at some shows, the Beatles had to play inside a six-foot-high cage.

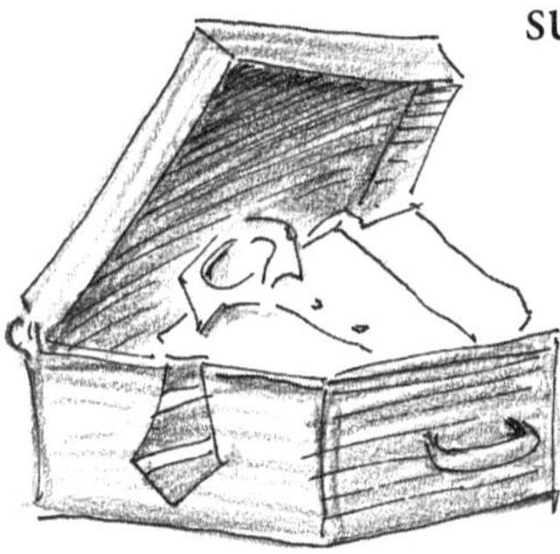

When they were on tour, the Beatles had to leave their families behind. John found this especially hard. He had a wife and a baby son. John barely had a chance to see them.

What if they didn't play any more concerts? What if they spent their time creating new music in the studio? Brian didn't like the idea. He wanted them to continue playing concerts so they could continue making a lot of money. But the Beatles had other ideas. They were tired of traveling. Instead of sightseeing, they spent most of their time running away from fans who wanted hugs, kisses, and autographs. They couldn't even go to the movies or to a restaurant anymore.

After one concert, fans chased down the band's limousine and shook it back and forth, hoping to get a peek at one of the band members. Luckily, John, Paul, George, and Ringo had faked them out. The boys had sneaked away secretly and were hiding inside an ambulance.

This may sound fun, but it wasn't. Even performing was a drag now. There were no more shows at small clubs. The Beatles were filling

baseball stadiums with fans. As the four of them stood on a small, square stage, as many as fifty thousand people would be screaming so loudly

that the Beatles couldn't hear themselves play. They had to guess when to start a song, and they made lots of mistakes.

"It was wrecking our playing," Ringo said. "The noise of the people just drowned everything."

John and Paul had other reasons to be fed up. They were growing into wonderful songwriters. They kept coming up with new ideas that they wanted to try out. But the fans going to their concerts only wanted to hear the old hits, the songs they knew the words to.

Against Brian's wishes, the Beatles began to spend more time in the studio. Their early songs had been very simple. "She Loves You" and "I Want to Hold Your Hand" were fast, happy tunes with words that everybody understood. The newer songs were different.

The first dramatic change came on "Yesterday," a song Paul said he heard in his head during a dream. The song is sad, about lost love. Paul's voice is supported by a quartet of classical musicians. "Yesterday" became one of the group's most popular songs when it was released in 1965. Since then, more than three thousand other musicians have recorded the song—a record reported by the *Guinness Book of World Records*.

In 1965 and 1966, the Beatles recorded *Rubber Soul* and *Revolver*. These albums were very different musically from their earlier ones. On one song, George used a sitar, which is an eight-hundred-year-old instrument. On another, Paul hired a saxophonist and a trumpet player. And on "Tomorrow Never Knows," some of the guitar music was prerecorded and then played backward on the album. The words to some of the songs were also strange and different. People are still trying to figure out what they mean. But the Beatles couldn't play

a song like "Tomorrow Never Knows" in concert. It was too complicated.

Brian kept forcing them to go back out on tour. The Beatles tried, but it didn't work. They were unhappy, and decided once and for all to stop doing concert tours. The last concert came on August 29, 1966, in San Francisco. Brian was upset. He was worried that rock bands that didn't play concerts could not stay popular. Other people were confused. Rumors

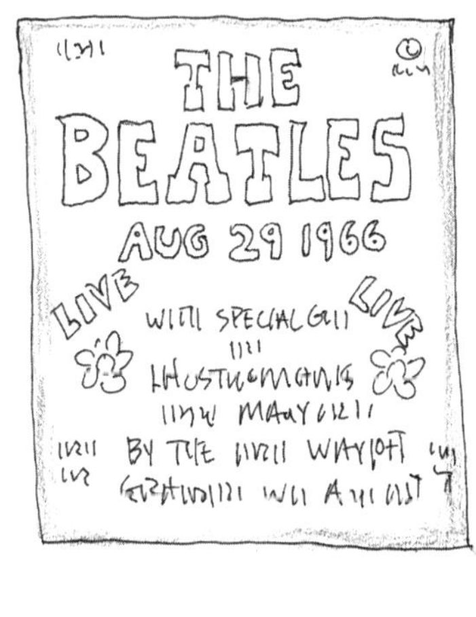

spread that the Beatles had broken up. George's mother, Louise, answered hundreds of letters from sad fans. The Beatles were not quitting, she wrote. They just had a new album to make.

Back at home, the Beatles had more freedom. They got married, and spent some time with their families. They went to art shows and even to the movies again. But most of all, they made music. They tried new types of songs. They hired a symphony to play along on a single recording.

They took more time than ever before to record albums. The world was changing. And so was their music. They had started in bands in the late '50s. It was a safer, simpler time. By the late 1960s, many young people were angry at the world their parents had made. They were

angry about the U.S. government waging war in Vietnam. They were angry about how African-Americans were treated. They were angry at big companies for polluting the planet.

Folksingers such as Bob Dylan and Joan Baez were writing powerful protest songs. The Beatles wrote these types of songs, too. They sang "All You Need Is Love" on national TV. For the song, they gathered in a circle with lots of friends, held hands, and repeated one word over and over: "love." Another song, "Revolution," started with a loud guitar and screaming as the Beatles sang angrily about people who started wars.

THE VIETNAM WAR

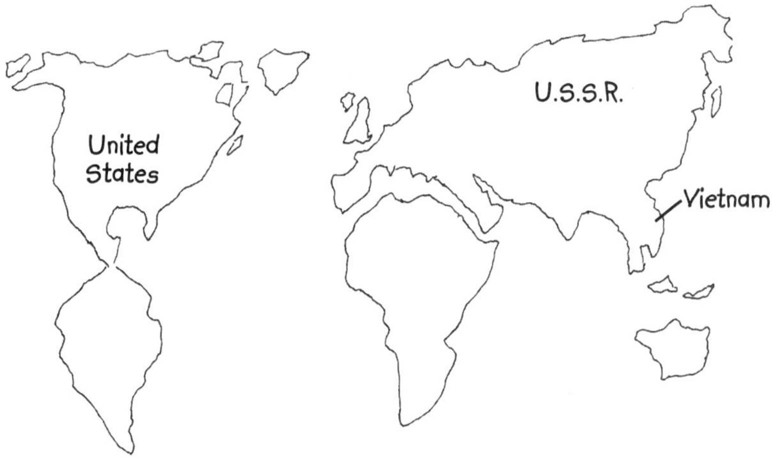

WHY DID THE U.S. GOVERNMENT SEND SOLDIERS TEN THOUSAND MILES AWAY TO VIETNAM?

VIETNAM WAS SEPARATED INTO SOUTH VIETNAM AND NORTH VIETNAM. THE GOVERNMENT IN NORTH VIETNAM WAS COMMUNIST. SOUTH VIETNAM WAS NOT COMMUNIST.

AT THAT TIME, THE BIGGEST ENEMY OF THE UNITED STATES WAS A COMMUNIST NATION—THE SOVIET UNION—WHICH HOPED TO SPREAD COMMUNISM TO OTHER COUNTRIES. THE UNITED STATES WANTED TO KEEP SOUTH VIETNAM FROM BECOMING COMMUNIST.

BY 1964, THOUSANDS OF SOLDIERS WERE FIGHTING IN VIETNAM. THE WAR DRAGGED ON FOR YEARS. MORE THAN FIFTY THOUSAND AMERICAN SOLDIERS DIED BEFORE IT ENDED. AND NORTH VIETNAM WON. IT TOOK OVER SOUTH VIETNAM AND IS STILL A COMMUNIST COUNTRY TODAY.

In 1967, a year after quitting the road, the Beatles released what many people think is their greatest album, *Sgt. Pepper's Lonely Hearts Club Band*. What made *Sgt. Pepper* so special is how the Beatles used so many different styles of music on one album. John sparked controversy with the song "Lucy in the Sky with Diamonds." People thought John was writing about LSD, a drug some people were using. Others couldn't figure out John's lyrics. But even the people who didn't understand the words could agree: The song was fun to listen to.

THE SIXTIES

WHEN THE BEATLES WERE JUST KIDS, YOUNG PEOPLE WANTED TO BE JUST LIKE THEIR PARENTS. THIS WAS THE 1950S. ALTHOUGH AMERICAN SOLDIERS WERE FIGHTING A WAR IN KOREA, THE WORLD SEEMED MUCH MORE PEACEFUL THAN IT HAD DURING WORLD WAR II. KIDS STUDIED HARD SO THEY COULD GO TO COLLEGE AND GET A GOOD JOB. BOYS WORE

BUTTON-DOWN SHIRTS AND SLACKS. GIRLS WORE LONG SKIRTS AND BOBBY SOCKS.

EVERYTHING CHANGED IN THE 1960S. PRESIDENT JOHN F. KENNEDY WAS SHOT AND KILLED. HIS BROTHER ROBERT WAS SHOT AND KILLED. DR. MARTIN LUTHER KING, JR., WAS SHOT AND KILLED. THE WAVE OF VIOLENCE SHOCKED EVERYONE. THE WORLD DIDN'T SEEM SAFE.

THE VIETNAM WAR GOT BIGGER. YOUNG PEOPLE WERE DRAFTED INTO THE ARMY. MANY DID NOT BELIEVE IN THE WAR, YET THEY HAD TO GO AND FIGHT. YOUNG AFRICAN-AMERICANS WERE TIRED OF WAITING TO BE TREATED LIKE WHITE PEOPLE. THEY WANTED THINGS TO CHANGE NOW. YOUNG PEOPLE, BLACK AND WHITE, GREW THEIR HAIR AND WORE CLOTHES THEIR PARENTS HATED. BOB DYLAN SAID, "DON'T TRUST ANYONE OVER THIRTY." AND MANY KIDS DIDN'T.

Chapter 9
The Beginning of the End

In the beginning, the Beatles loved being a band. They loved being famous. They went from being four poor teenagers to world stars. Fans adored them. And they had more money than they could ever hope to spend.

John bought a Rolls-Royce. It had a television and refrigerator in it. Paul also bought a fancy car, an Aston Martin. George got a house and had painters decorate it with flowers. "When the money first began to pour in, I'd go and buy ten suits, a dozen shirts, and three cars," Ringo said. "I spent money like it had just been invented."

As time passed, they began to see the sour side of being so successful—of being the Beatles. They were expected to spend all of their time together. They were friends, sure, but they were getting older. They had families now, and didn't want to just hang out with the guys. So, slowly, they started to drift apart. They were already dressing differently. The times were changing. It would have been silly for the Beatles to show up in their matching, collarless suits. The Beatles made sure to keep up with the latest styles. John let his hair grow long. He also grew a thick beard. He took to wearing a white suit. George and Ringo grew mustaches. Paul tried growing one, though he didn't keep it for long. They wore clothes with lots of style and lots of colors. This is how the hippies dressed.

The band had done about 20 albums, more than 220 songs. Their next project was to record an album and make a movie at the same time. The idea

was to show the world how the group worked so well together. Instead, *Let It Be* showed how tired the Beatles were of one another. Paul wanted to start playing concerts again. But nobody else did. George wanted more of his songs to appear on the album. The other Beatles said no. John wanted his new wife, Yoko Ono, at the recording studio all the time. The others didn't want her there.

Yoko Ono was an "experimental" artist. She wasn't interested in drawing pretty pictures of flowers, or of horses running through mountain streams. Her artwork was unusual. Very unusual. For example, she once made a film of a fly walking up and down a naked person's body. Yoko also had very strong opinions. She thought the other Beatles should listen to John more.

During the recording of *Let It Be*, Yoko sat next to John. She listened to the band discuss how to play the music. When there was a disagreement, she would whisper in John's ear, or give her opinion

to the group. She loved John, and always took his side. The other Beatles thought that outsiders—even wives—didn't belong in the studio. It had always been just the four of them there.

Let It Be turned into a big mess. By the end, the Beatles were barely talking to one another. They couldn't finish the album. When the movie was released, almost no one went to see it. The Beatles didn't even show up for the opening.

Paul felt bad. He didn't want the band to break up like this. Yes, they had grown apart. But they still cared about one another. Paul convinced his bandmates to make one more album. This time, he said, there would be no fighting. It would be just like the old days. And it was.

They named that album *Abbey Road*, after the address of their recording studio. Everyone—even Ringo, who didn't have a very good voice—got a chance to sing. The album was released and almost immediately it went to number one on the charts.

Critics everywhere raved about its beauty.

Then news came that stunned the world: It was over. The Beatles were breaking up.

Chapter 10
Everyone Is Going Solo

It was 1970. And they were no longer a band. But they were still musicians and still famous.

Paul wanted to spend time with his family. He and his wife, Linda, whom he married in 1969, bought a farm in Scotland. They had three children. (One daughter, Stella, grew up to be a famous fashion designer.)

Paul made a solo album called *McCartney*. He played every instrument himself, including guitar, drums, and piano. Soon he started another band, called Wings, and played concerts again, which he had always loved. Paul taught Linda, who was a photographer, how to play the keyboard for his band. That way, they would never have to be apart.

George and Ringo were also busy making music. Paul and John had always been the lead songwriters in the Beatles. George and Ringo weren't allowed to sing much. Now, they could make their own albums. George had so many songs saved up that when he recorded his album, it was longer than any of the ones released by the Beatles. In

1971, with his song "My Sweet Lord," he became the first Beatle to have a number-one hit as a solo artist. George also cared a lot about helping people in need. Once, he organized a giant concert to raise money for starving children in Bangladesh. He also produced movies, including Monty Python's *Life of Brian*.

One thing about George never changed, no matter how famous he was. He was still shy. Even after all the tours, he was afraid to go onstage. He always had to be coaxed into playing publicly. He eventually bought a one-hundred-room mansion in England with his second wife, Olivia, and their son, Dhani. A tall fence around it gave the family some privacy. It didn't always keep out strangers, though. In 1999, a man broke into their mansion. George was stabbed, but he recovered, and the man was arrested.

Ringo wasn't as successful a musician as George. Still, he loved being famous because it meant people would always laugh at his jokes, invite him to parties, and ask him to play concerts. He never liked arguing with his bandmates. Now he was happy to be at peace again. Ringo didn't have a good singing voice. His speaking voice, though, was very entertaining—particularly for younger fans.

Ringo narrated a popular children's television show, *Thomas the Tank Engine & Friends*, and played Mr. Conductor on *Shining Time Station*.

In 1973 and 1974, Ringo had number-one hits with "Photograph" and "You're Sixteen." He formed the All Starr Band, which continues to tour. In 2010, the year he turned seventy, Ringo came out with a new album called *Y Not*.

John was probably the most glad to be free of the Beatles. Now he could say whatever he wanted about politics. He and Yoko visited the United States often. John spoke out against the Vietnam War, and people listened. He recorded a beautiful antiwar song called "Give Peace a Chance." He and Yoko held many protests, where they explained why they thought the war should end. Instead of a "be-in" (a large gathering of people), they held a "bed-in." They wore pajamas and stayed in bed for eight days as a protest. John and Yoko also rented big billboards that said: "War Is Over! (If You Want It.)"

The American government wasn't happy about this. One senator from South Carolina, Strom Thurmond, wanted John kicked out of the country. The FBI started to follow John around, watching everything he did.

Did John run back to England? No. He and Yoko moved permanently to the United States in 1971. They bought an apartment in the Dakota, a famous building in New York City. They would live there the rest of John's life.

So as John, Paul, George, and Ringo lived their lives apart from one another, one big question remained: When would the Beatles get back together?

Never, was the answer, John said. Some of them did work together, but never all four at the same time. George played with John and Ringo on their albums. Ringo played on John's, on Paul's, and on George's albums. Paul played on George's and on Ringo's albums. And John played on

George's and on Ringo's albums.

Why didn't the group ever have a reunion? Mainly because John and Paul were too mad at each other.

In fact, after the Beatles broke up, John and Paul said hurtful things about each other in public. John even made fun of Paul's new music in the song "How Do You Sleep?"

In 1972, two years after the breakup, John and Paul started talking again. And there was one night that they almost performed. It was in 1975, on a Saturday night, when Paul happened to be in New York City. He went over to John's apartment, and they watched some TV.

The comedy show *Saturday Night Live* was on. Strangely, that night, the show's producers offered to pay the Beatles one thousand dollars each if they would reunite for the program. It was a joke.

People in the audience laughed because the Beatles had already been offered more than a million dollars to play together again. Paul and John thought it would be funny to show up at the television studio and surprise everyone. In the end, they stayed in John's apartment. But fans still talk about what it would have been like had they sung together one more time.

Chapter 11
The Saddest Day

By the mid-1970s, John Lennon was still one of the most famous people in the world, more so than the other Beatles. Was he happy? No.

He was still a young man—only in his mid-thirties. Yet he'd spent so much time in the spotlight. He never seemed at ease with himself, even at home. His marriage to Yoko Ono was breaking up. John was afraid it would end in divorce, just as his first marriage had. Eventually, Yoko asked John to move out. He agreed, though he didn't want to. John began to drink too much. He also took drugs. He started hanging out with people who only wanted to go to parties. He got into fights. His music suffered.

Yoko reconsidered and asked John to come

home. A few months later, Yoko told him she was going to have a baby. On October 9, 1975, they had a baby boy and named him Sean.

When John's first son, Julian, was born, in 1963, John had been on tour a lot. This time he would be a different kind of father. John wanted to stay home with Sean. He would learn how to change diapers. He would be there to see his baby's first steps. "From now on, my chief responsibility is my family," he told reporters.

For him, that meant quitting music. John didn't record any albums or play a single concert while Sean was a baby. He was there in the morning when Sean woke up. He dressed Sean and played with him all day. John even learned to cook. He called his half sister on the phone to tell her about his first try at baking bread. He did such a bad job that when he tried to cut it, the knife bent.

For five years, John almost never left his apartment. Music was still on his mind, though. Every once in a while a new song would pop into his head. Not wanting to forget it, John would sit at his piano and play the song into a small tape recorder. Then he put the tape away for later.

Lots of people, including other musicians, urged him to play concerts again, or record. He kept saying no. But then suddenly, unexpectedly, he changed his mind. It wasn't because he needed the money. He was rich. It wasn't for attention. He had plenty of that.

The reason John decided to go back was simply because he loved making music. It was a part of him that he couldn't ignore anymore. So when

Sean was turning five and ready to start school, John went back to work.

He didn't sign any recording contracts. He didn't hold a big concert. First, he needed to practice. He wrote and played test songs, or "demos," by laying a tape recorder on top of his piano. Before long, he had more than enough songs for an album.

The next step was to make the album. John started recording and asked Yoko to sing some songs on it, too, even though he knew many of his fans would be upset. He called their album *Double Fantasy*. Some of the songs John recorded—"Watching the Wheels" and "(Just Like) Starting Over"—were about taking a break from music. Others were about his family. He wrote one about Sean called "Beautiful Boy," and one about Yoko called "Woman."

The album came out on November 15, 1980, and was a big success. It sold five hundred thousand copies in two weeks. John was excited, and looked forward to producing more music.

Then, on December 8, 1980, something happened that nobody alive at the time will ever forget.

That afternoon, John and Yoko were walking outside their apartment on Central Park West. A man named Mark David Chapman came up and asked John to autograph his album. John liked doing this for fans. But Mark

David Chapman wasn't like other fans. He was mentally ill. He heard voices in his head, voices that told him to hurt John Lennon.

That evening, Chapman returned. He waited near the entrance of the Dakota. When John and Yoko arrived home, Chapman called out, "Mr. Lennon." Then he took out a gun and fired. John Lennon, who hated violence, who didn't believe in the use of guns, fell to the ground. He died shortly after. He was only forty years old.

The world was stunned.

New Yorkers came from all over the city to stand outside John's home. Some were in their pajamas, crying. They left flowers. Strangers hugged one another. They sang John's songs.

Six days later, more than one hundred thousand people gathered in Central Park. There were ten minutes of silence. Then, John's song "Imagine"

played over loudspeakers. The song was his dream of peace: "Imagine all the people/Living life in peace."

John's death was a terrible tragedy. But it wasn't the end of what he stood for.

He is remembered not only as a Beatle, but for trying to make a better world. In Central Park in New York City there is a mosaic circle with the word "Imagine."

It is a memorial to John Lennon. In 2010, thirty years after his death, huge crowds came—as they do every year on December 8—and left flowers for John. "Imagine" remains a song for peace. That's why Neil Young chose to sing the song on television just days after the 9/11 terrorist attacks.

Fifteen years after John's death, the three other

Beatles did reunite. Remember those songs John wrote while Sean was a baby? Yoko had the demo tapes. She let Paul, George, and Ringo record their voices and instruments along with John's. In 1996, the first song, "Free as a Bird," went straight to number one on the charts.

Paul, George, and Ringo continued their separate careers. There were sad times ahead. Paul's wife, Linda, died in 1998. Their marriage had been a very happy one. Paul remarried in 2002 but split up four years later. Then George announced terrible news. He had cancer. He died in 2001.

A year to the day of his death, Paul and Ringo gathered for a tribute concert to him in London's Royal Albert Hall. They played George's songs with other famous musicians and with George's son, Dhani, who was twenty-four at the time. The concert could have been very sad. After all, the musicians had lost one of their oldest, dearest

friends. But instead, they were cheered by playing George's songs. At the end of the concert, flower petals slowly floated down from above, onto the stage.

To this day, the Beatles remain the most famous musical group in the world. Their songs have been recorded by everyone from legendary crooner Frank Sinatra to pop musicians such as U2 and Elliott Smith. In 2000, a Beatles greatest hits collection called *1* went straight to the top of the charts—even though none of the songs was new.

The Beatles are gone. John is gone. George is gone now, too. But not the music. That will live forever.

TIMELINE OF THE BEATLES' LIVES

1940 — John Lennon and Richard Starkey—later known as Ringo Starr—are born in Liverpool, England

1942 — Paul McCartney is born

1943 — George Harrison is born

1956 — Paul sees John's band, the Quarrymen, play at a church function; he's asked to join the group after trying out

1957 — Paul introduces George to John; George becomes a member of the band

1960 — The group changes its name from the Quarrymen to the Beatles

1962 — Ringo replaces Pete Best to become the new Beatles drummer

1963 — The Beatles release their first album, *Please Please Me*; it's a big hit in England but doesn't do well in the United States

1964 — Finally popular in the United States, the Beatles play *The Ed Sullivan Show* and are watched by seventy-three million Americans; the band's movie, *A Hard Day's Night*, is released; the British Invasion has begun

1965 — The song "Yesterday" becomes a number-one hit; "Yesterday" will eventually be recorded by three thousand other musicians, a world record

Tired of touring, the Beatles play their last concert; John meets Yoko Ono for the first time; they'll fall in love and get married — **1966**

Sgt. Pepper's Lonely Hearts Club Band is released; it is immediately hailed as one of the greatest albums ever — **1967**

As part of recording *Let It Be*, the Beatles perform for a few friends on the roof of a building—the last time they will play in public together; they are forced to stop when somebody complains to the police — **1969**

Paul announces the Beatles are breaking up — **1970**

After his son Sean is born, John decides to stop making music for a few years — **1975**

John, who has just released his first album in five years, is killed by a disturbed fan; more than one hundred thousand people gather in New York's Central Park to mourn — **1980**

Paul, George, and Ringo use a tape of John singing a demo to record the first new Beatles song since they broke up; "Free As a Bird" goes straight to number one — **1996**

George dies of cancer — **2001**

TIMELINE OF THE WORLD

1941 — United States joins Allied forces in World War II

1945 — Nazi Germany surrenders and Adolf Hitler commits suicide

1951 — The first color TV is sold

1955 — Rosa Parks, an African-American, refuses to move from a seat near the front of a bus in Birmingham, Alabama; this brings national attention to the Civil Rights Movement

1956 — Elvis Presley sparks controversy with his suggestive dancing on *The Ed Sullivan Show*

1961 — The Berlin Wall is built, dividing the city into democratic West Berlin and communist East Berlin

1963 — President John F. Kennedy is assassinated by Lee Harvey Oswald; Lyndon Johnson becomes president

1964 — Boxer Muhammad Ali becomes heavyweight champion

1965 — Vietnam War grows bigger, as the United States sends more troops

1966 — Protests against draft and Vietnam War; hippies beginning to gather to listen to music and call for peace

Civil rights leader Martin Luther King, Jr. and presidential candidate Robert F. Kennedy are assassinated	1968
Neil Armstrong becomes first man on the moon; three-day Woodstock music festival attracts four hundred thousand people to Bethel, New York, for an outdoor event that's the biggest of the hippie era	1969
United States decides to leave Vietnam	1973
President Richard M. Nixon resigns because of Watergate scandal	1974
First "test tube" baby born through artificial insemination	1978
Sandra Day O'Connor becomes the first woman appointed to the Supreme Court	1981
The Berlin Wall falls as Germany is unified	1989
Collapse of the Soviet Union	1991
Bertrand Piccard and Brian Jones become first to ride around the world in a hot-air balloon	1999
World Trade Center in New York City is destroyed by terrorists	2001

BIBLIOGRAPHY

Baird, Julia, and Geoffrey Guiliano. **John Lennon: My Brother.** Henry Holt & Co, 1st American edition, 1988.

Bowles, Jerry G. **A Thousand Sundays: The Story of the Ed Sullivan Show.** Putnam, New York, 1980.

Coleman, Ray. **The Man Who Made the Beatles: An Intimate Biography of Brian Epstein.** McGraw-Hill, New York, 1989.

Crossaperback, Craig. **Beatles-discography.com: Day-by-day Song-by-song Record-by-record.** IUniverse, 2004.

Davies, Hunter. **The Beatles, (2nd Rev edition).** W. W. Norton & Company, New York, 2004.

Giuliano, Geoffrey. **Dark Horse: The Life and Art of George Harrison.** Da Capo Press, New York, 1997.

Giuliano, Geoffrey. **The Lost Beatles Interviews.** Cooper Square Press, New York, 2002.

Hertsgaard, Mark. **A Day in the Life: The Music and Artistry of the Beatles.** Delta, 1996.

Lennon, John. **Imagine: A Celebration of John Lennon.** Studio, 1st American edition, 1995.

Lennon, John, and Yoko Ono, David Sheff, and G. Barry Golson. **The Playboy Interviews with John Lennon and Yoko Ono.** Berkley Publishing Group, New York, 1982.

Leonard, John, and Claudia Falkenburg and Andrew Solt, eds. **Really Big Show: A Visual History of The Ed Sullivan Show.** Studio, 1992.

Miles, Barry. **Paul McCartney: Many Years from Now.** Henry Holt & Company, New York, 1998.

Partridge, Elizabeth. **This Land Was Made for You and Me: The Life and Songs of Woody Guthrie.** Viking, New York, 2002.

Shipper, Mark. **Paperback Writer: The Life and Times of the Beatles, the Spurious Chronicle of Their Rise to Stardom, Their Triumphs and Disasters.** Ace Books, New York, 1978.

Shotton, Pete, and Nicholas Schaffner. **John Lennon: In My Life.** Stein & Day Pub, Michigan, 1983.

Sulpy, Doug, and Ray Schweighardt. **Get Back: The Unauthorized Chronicle of the Beatles' Let It Be Disaster.** St. Martin's Press, New York, 1999.